Critical Acclaim

T0149841

"Gervais weaves an anecdot. ... ue to knit through the reader's imagination long after the book has been put away."

Canadian Literature

"...for him, the act of making a poem or telling a story is an act of faith, so that observances of the commonplace become moments of transcendent epiphany and insight, rather than merely journalistic jottings or diaries"

The Oxford Companion to Canadian Literature.

"The best of Marty Gervais' work creates an engaging tension between the ordinary surfaces of life and the underlying pathos...

The Globe and Mail

"...Gervais doesn't strike me as a particularly "literary" poet. I mean his concerns are with human feelings, laughter, what happens inside the brain when certain lights are turned on. He strikes me as honest...I mean there's no phoniness...no pretensions..."

Al Purdy, Governor General's Award Winner

"Over the span of a fifty-year career, in poems that are delightful and memorable, Marty Gervais is one of the finest poetic voices in Canada. His powerful and cleat reportage, his keen eye for the unusual in the everyday, and his delight in our humanity affirm Gervais as an essential chronicler of our beautiful souls."

Bruce Meyer, renowned Author and Poet, CBC Broadcaster

Nothing more Perfect

Poems

Marty Gervais

Library and Archives Canada Cataloguing in Publication

Title: Nothing more perfect / Marty Gervais.

Names: Gervais, C. H. (Charles Henry), 1946- author.

Description: Poems.

Identifiers: Canadiana (print) 20210169257
            Canadiana (ebook) 20210169273

ISBN 9781771615600 (softcover) ISBN 9781771615617 (PDF)
ISBN 9781771615624 (EPUB) ISBN 9781771615631 (Kindle)

Classification: LCC PS8563.E7 N68 2021
                DDC C811/.54—dc23

Published by Mosaic Press, Oakville, Ontario, Canada, 2021.

MOSAIC PRESS, Publishers
www.Mosaic-Press.com
Copyright © Marty Gervais

Printed and bound in Canada.

MOSAIC PRESS
1252 Speers Road, Units 1 & 2, Oakville, Ontario, L6L 5N9
(905) 825-2130 • info@mosaic-press.com • www.mosaic-press.com

A Selection of Book Titles by Marty Gervais

Non-fiction

The Rumrunners (Firefly Books), 1980
Seeds in the Wilderness: Profile of Religious Leaders (Quarry Press, 1994).
From America Sent: Letters to Henry Miller (Quarry Press, 1995).
Reno (A Novel), (Mosaic Press, 1996)
My Town: Faces of Windsor (Biblioasis Books), 2006
The Rumrunners: A Scrapbook of Prohibition (Biblioasis Books), 2007
Ghost Road and Other Forgotten Stories of Windsor (Biblioasis Books) 2012

Poetry

A Sympathy Orchestra (Fiddlehead Books) 1970
Poems for American Daughters (Porcupine's Quill) 1976
The Believable Body (Fiddlehead Books) 1979
Up Country Lines (Penumbra Books) 1979
Into A Blue Morning: Selected Poems, with introduction by Al Purdy (Hounslow Press) 1982
Letters from the Equator Penumbra Press, 1986.
Scenes from the Present: New Selected Poems Penumbra Press, 1991
Playing God Mosaic Press, 1994..
Tearing Into a Summer Day Mosaic Press, 1996.
The Science of Nothing (Mosaic Press, 2000).
To Be Now: New and Selected Poems (Mosaic Press, 2003).
Table Manners (Selected and New Poems 2014-2018 (Mosaic Press, 2018)
Nine Lives: A Reunion in Paris (Urban Farmhouse Press, 2020)

For Donna

Table of Contents

NOTHING MORE PERFECT

Love is our true destiny. We do not find the meaning of life by ourselves alone – we find it with another.

Thomas Merton
Monk, Poet

One day I realized the world was open to me. I realized all of the possibilities that could exist for me...all of the images that I could capture, all the lives I could enter, all the people I could meet and how much I could learn from them ...

Mary Ellen Mark
Photographer

Preface
By Bruce Meyer

What makes life worth living are its perfect moments, those fragments of reality that break free from the dross, the blur, and often the pain of existence, and punctuate it with a memorable clarity that proves joy is real. Those are the moments a person wants to carry with them into the afterlife. Those are the perceptions that remind us of what we are doing here and how important it is that we live and find love in the small experiences that are so easily lost.

Nothing more Perfect is a volume of poems that could easily be called a book of selected joys. As Thomas Merton aptly put is in the epigraph to this collection, "We do not find meaning by ourselves alone – we find it with another." In these poems, Marty Gervais presents a catalogue of those moments of meaning. From the planting tulips with his wife to anticipating his daughter's birth, Gervais asserts the importance of those moments that go missing from much of literature.

Poetry, especially contemporary verse, loves to dwell on the emphatic, on the shocking and painful realities that awaken us to the world and what we must do to live in it. But there are other moments as well, moments when we simply live. What often slips through the cracks of the contemporary poetic idiom are those little instances of realization of what it means to be human. Too often, poetry shouts. It waves placards. It brandishes causes, and it forgets that life goes on even if poets are not recording it. I am reminded of W.H. Auden's poem, "Musee des Beaux

Arts," where the poet describes paintings in a Belgian gallery by the early northern Renaissance painter, Pietr Breughel the Elder. Auden argues that it is not the grand gesture that is important but the small details of life, the dog that scratches its behind on a tree as the "Slaughter of the Innocents" takes place or the image of a boy falling from the sky whose precipitous drop into the sea is over-shadowed by the man ploughing his field or the beautiful golden ship sailing into a sunset. Likewise, the often-over-looked American poet, Jack Gilbert, writes in "The Abnor-mal Is Not Courage," that human strength resides in the long marriage rather than just the rapturous honeymoon, and concludes and courage is "the normal excellence of long accomplishment." What Auden and Gilbert say about courage and the details of life are what Gervais champions.

When I read these poems, I am reminded of the rarity of interior paintings. Several Danish painters of the Nine-teenth century, among them the gifted Vilehelm Hammer-shói, gave us a unique insight into what life is really like. There is nothing earth-shattering in his interiors. They are serene, beautiful, calm, and very, very real. His small rooms, his exacting depictions of life as most of life is, are, to my mind, stunning and far more important than land-scapes with no one in them or great slabs of ice crushing a ship. They are also the most difficult canvases to paint. There are no tricks permitted. There are no grand state-ments being made, no kings presented for inspection. They are life. Gervais has not let life slip between his fingers. In all these poems he reminds us of what it means to be us.

The interior world, the world of daily life, is a chal-lenging subject, perhaps more challenging and demanding than writing about huge topics, less colorful than rugged landscapes, and perhaps and at first glance less important than human beings caught up in maelstroms of history.

The poets who write about such things are important, too, and have their place, but they do not say everything that could be said or salvaged of us. They do not sing of the ordinary, and it is the ordinary that is the hardest thing to write about. The Canadian-British poet, David Wevill, once wrote, "The hardest thing to imagine is yourself." And though it is hard for us to imagine ourselves as we really are, this is exactly what Gervais accomplishes in this book.

Most of us will never know what it means (I hope) to be caught in the webs and snares of enormous world-altering moments. Most of us, however, will know what it is like to look outside our windows and watch the rain or wonder what to do with an abandoned robin's nest. This interior poetry is harder to write than the poetry of grandiose topics. Interior poetry demands that the poet understand human nature in its most delicate and fragile manifestation. This is the art of Marty Gervais.

Gervais is a poet who questions everything. He wants to know what makes reality work. As a newspaper reporter, he covered events, large and small. He spoke to giants of his time and he interviewed those who simply led their lives and who were happy that someone took interest in something they did. His articles with the giants are insightful and fun to read, but his interviews with people celebrating a milestone in their lives, people doing unique things that despite their uniqueness were not out of the realm of the ordinary — the human being engaged in the challenge of being human in a quiet, introspective manner — took tremendous skill to elicit and record.

The great artists, I assert, are not those who study the deaths of fallen kings, but those who watched and wondered at the mighty and then went on with their own lives. For Gervais, the poetry is in the aftermath. In saying this, the title of the book seems completely apropos. There is nothing more perfect than those moments when we not only feel love or recognize ourselves in others, as the philosopher Emmanuel Levinas pointed out when he said that the face of the divine is worn by every human being, but when we forget ourselves in the act of being ourselves. I can think of nothing more perfect and nothing more important than the self which forgets itself yet recognizes the complexity, the beauty, the wonder of a moment, and records it so the lives we live are not swept away by Time.

Bruce Meyer

Rescued Tulips

I made the mistake this spring
of helping in the garden by raking up
the showering of cedar needles
from trees along the fence

and in my enthusiasm to please
somehow dislodged a cluster of tulips
my wife rescued and placed
in a water-filled glass that now sits

on our breakfast table for me
and I study the tulips slowly opening
breathing in the clutter and chaos
of our urban dwelling, not a natural

place for a tulip to thrive
yet they're here to complete their moment
to tell me nothing can be done
to make things better
so *Move out of the way, get a life...*

In Her Mother's House

She lives in her mother's house, leaning
casually against the bathroom sink, brushing
her teeth, every night the same routine, an ordinary
pale green toothbrush patiently working
its perfect way along gleaming
incisors, cuspids, and molars

and she is daydreaming in the mirror
seeing the same person every night
and it reminds me of the way she pauses
in the garden, a tin watering can, holding it
high to one side, sprinkling tap water
over chrysanthemums and daylilies and hostas

and the person she imagines is her mother
who in the first days of May would step out
like any good mother, step out into the yard
the same yard, to greet the new shoots of life
sprouting for eager air and sunshine
on the first warm days of spring

Morning of our Anniversary

for Donna, Nov. 7, 2020

There was frost on the windows in
the high-ceiling rooms and snow covered
the trees and alleys that led down
to the park and beyond

and you were asleep, curled in the warmth
of a new day breaking and nothing
could be better than this, where I sat
watching the sun tiptoeing back to life

and maybe I knew nothing of us back then
of our future, that moment stretching out
but here I am again, 50 years later
rising early waiting for the sun

waiting for you, and I have no idea
of how to finish these words, what to say
— it is enough to watch you sleep
assured there's nothing more perfect

A Dance of Self-Isolation

I danced alone in the sunlight
at the back of the house my first day
out of the hospital after acute kidney
failure, my first day of isolation
that I call freedom, and ahead of me
three months of winter, moving from
one space to another in the house
following the shift of sunlight, its warmth
through the cold windows, snow
covering the ground just beyond
and I moved slowly, more a pantomime
of a silly dance, my ailing body pretending
to lift and move, my limbs shrunken
practicing this painful grace yearning
to blossom in this routine of hope

and just when I was ready to embrace
the business that I once knew —
the world around me began to settle
into this mandated routine of social distancing
self-isolation and working from home
and back I went, retreating to the comfort
of my rooms trailing the sun again
eager for its warmth as I stood and stared
out the south window of my house
to marvel at the magnolia tree
that stretched alive in budding colour
playing its own crazy pantomime of dance

After Eye Surgery

I know you're there —
your presence imperceptible
on this cool summer night
windows open
nightjars and owls
in the nearby Blue Spruce
a passing car
a whirring of a neighbour's bicycle

I have gone to bed early
sore eyes feeling a cloud of
Tylenol and Ativan bearing me
across a dreamy landscape

memories of the sun settling down
like a tired old man across Burgundy fields
the sudden glimpse of a red fox leaping
over solitary bales of hay

I know you're there, feel your hand
upon my back the fading daytime
slipping out the door and windows
leaving only you and me
and we don't need to speak
I know you're there

Nov. 7, 2018

for Donna

The dashboard panel lit up
and it was *Hey Jude* navigating us through
the darkness and your car curving
with each bend in the night road
this early and windy autumn with
looming shadows following us
back from the Point

I knew nothing about you
I knew everything

Nothing in this darkness
but my words tangled in the spiraling
cigarette smoke caressing the features
of your face, blond hair and tailored black coat

I wanted to know everything
I wanted to know nothing

The music telling me I have found her
Now go and get her
Remember to let her into your heart

Everything so clear as this car moved
with grace and lightness
the melody rising into promises
into letting go and we are here
a half century of remembering
trusting the unknown and knowing everything

Raining Cats and Dogs

It rained cats and dogs, she said
and I tried to fix that in my mind
what that would be like if suddenly
the heavens opened and cats and dogs
started tumbling out of a sky

a sky so heavy, so black, so windswept
it really didn't make any sense
but I thought if it did what would
it be like in our city, all these animals
all sizes and colours, all breeds, all

temperament and behaviour, an
ecumenical assembly of God's creatures
all landing on our streets, a little stunned
and shaking from the sudden impact
of parachuting from the swirl of clouds

and running for safety up sheltered trees
or barking up a storm, and I am told
this was standard fare in medieval days
when not only did it rain cats and dogs
but also pitchforks sending troubled townspeople

rushing for cover holding on to their hats
fighting with their inverted umbrellas
but it wasn't just cats and dogs and pitchforks
— an 18th Century English playwright
asked what about the polecats that

swooped down from the thundering sky
and I ask my friend what will we do about
the cleanup, all these cats and dogs and polecats
swimming in the storm waters of our town
and she says it's simple — they'll make great pets

Everyday Worry

Early morning I retreat
to the backyard and feel the beginnings
of summer on my shoulders
and sit and drink tea, and realize
suddenly in the midst of all the flurry
of everyday news and worry
I am distracted by the tiniest of details

particularly this spider inching its way
across the thinnest of lines
maybe his own world is one of torment
fretting over a perilous passage
between two branches, the height
from the high grass far beneath this tree
clearly as steep as a skyscraper

Yet I imagine it may be so much
better for him, this Wallenda adventurer
avoiding the news, the talk, the panic
of every day as he spins his solitary magic
in the safety of a domain where the sun
praises him and where he thrives on risk
this footloose and confident soul

Let Me Go First

I don't want to mourn your death
Let me go first, free me of arrangements
solemnities, eulogies, loneliness, closets full of shoes
and dresses, jewelry, eyeglasses

Let me be the flattened bicycle tire
hanging from a nail in the garage
an abandoned, forgotten tennis racket
a winter tire leaning against a post
cardboard box of old vinyl records

I'd rather be those than be me
waiting to catch up, days spent writing
sappy sentimental poems to your memory

I know it's selfish but what else is new —
I was always first out the door
you always minutes late

I don't want to change things —
I just want to be first

P.S. I still love you

The Garden

What kind of a poet am I
that I know nothing about
plants and animals and stars
or even a summer sky that waves at me
for my attention like a young girl
with a kite on a beach

My world is urban — an everyday of houses
and factories and shopping malls
and highways and streetlights and buses

yet still the garden beyond the city window persists
calling me with a subtle and effortless breeze
coaxing me to look up from my keyboard

But what kind of poet am I
paying no heed to this seemingly ever-present chorus
of daylilies, marigolds, tulips, snapdragons,
daffodils, pansies, and begonias

None of which I know by name

My only relationship is to crank the lawnmower
and maneuver in and around these creatures
as in a busy downtown parking lot

I don't know anybody here

So what kind of poet am I
that I sail about my day sadly showing
no curiosity about these bright and beautiful faces

I don't see anybody here

Instead I stare at a keyboard's alphabet of tiny squares
that prattle of possibilities of past, present, and future
and maybe only then realize this is a garden plot
below a sky of mysteries and dreams
with each one stretching to be noticed
to dance and to be free

Maybe then I become the poet and venture into the garden
behind the city window and finally hear these lively
sons and daughters rising

I am the poet
I know everybody here
I am listening

I apologize

Who is this old Man?

for Virgil Wright

An old man in the hospital bed
twisted up, sunken cheeks, eyes agape —
maybe studying spidery cracks in the ceiling
or marveling at the network of ordinary light fixtures

his mind always stretching back to a hot Texas sun
— his youthfulness far gone
strength vanishing day by day
as he fixes upon something above him
something that might save him

A black & white photograph
affixed to the wall behind his bed
shows a young aerialist glorying in the circus
— the trapeze, he says, was like suddenly
catching the melody of an old-time tune
and in that instant he could sense spectators
rising from their seats with thunderous applause

If only they could hear what he hears
If only they could see what he sees

Whatever Happens

Whatever happens to things
that are certain but go missing
go elsewhere, find themselves
in other hands though
they were clearly meant for you

whenever things happen to find
themselves elsewhere when other
hands find the things that are clearly
meant for you though you made other

choices too late to change the way
things happen or feel the hands that
take away things clearly yours that
you find elsewhere when it's too late

Winter of Angels

Still dark and the first snow
softly falls as I step into the day
first light and a white glow catch
on the sleepy black oaks

angels, I think, this winter they come
telling me to walk, to breathe
to listen, to be silent and I hear
only my feet moving in the cold air

a winter of angels in pursuit as
I search for nothing but the silence
that comes with the morning
these ghosts of joyful silence

DECEMBER LIGHT

The Motel on Main Street

I was nearly 12, and wandered
by the u-shaped motel
that sat on the main drag
like an old aunt refusing to bid goodbye

I was taking a shortcut through the parking lot
making my way to a friend's
That's when I noticed a door ajar
in one of the units —

a sudden blur in the gloom of that room
a single light partly silhouetting a woman
slipping on a summer dress
over her head and down over bra and panties
hands smoothing out the cotton
momentarily looking up, spotting me
standing stock still in the lot
I want to think she just smiled and turned
escaping into darkness of the room
I continued my way to my friend's
but never forgot that instant —

Tonight, now 73 years old, I shuffle
into the cramped motel office
check in, ask for Room 106
and the hotel keeper hands me the key

I sit on the edge of the bed
coat and hat still on, slumped before a mirror
Why am I here? Maybe it's to gather

that moment into a bouquet
of darkness, of light, of beauty
something fraught and forsaken
and suddenly she is there —

or is that simply a mere gesture
of trailing light from a passing car

yet she is here, sitting beside me
leaning over to slip on her shoes
saying goodbye, summers long past
all of her now in a silhouette
brightening into a whisper of light

Hospital Supper

How can I complain —
Jell-O every day from the
hospital kitchen

my daily diet with Crohn's Disease

Red, orange, peach —
I call downstairs
Don't send me blueberry
— it looks too much
like anti-freeze

Then I read about
Adolph Eichmann's last meal

Eichmann ate nothing that day
but drank a half bottle of Israeli wine
and slowly wiped his face
with the back of his left hand

Eichmann wore his jailhouse slippers
to the gallows, refusing
to give them up

asked the executioner
to leave his glasses on

Tonight, I sleep with my glasses on
— untouched blueberry Jell-O
resting on the bedside table

December Light

I

December light through high windows
tells me I am in Lisbon
a rail station
waking up in near darkness

The nurse at the foot of my bed tells me otherwise

I am mistaken and I am going nowhere
I am in a ward with three other sick men

The December light tells me it is a cold day
better to huddle in a sea of white flannelette
submit to the regimen of everyday
temperature, blood pressure
the body poked and prodded
a catheter, tubes running off the edge of the bed

I am not in the warmth of Lisbon
December light winking from eyebrow-shaped windows
I am deceived — the trains aren't running
the ticket I have is going nowhere

The nurse straightens the blankets
whispers for me to go back to sleep
Instead, I study the light brightening
in the high windows

I am in a ward with three other men
This is not a train station
This is not Lisbon
Morning is hours away

I am going nowhere

2

I may have gotten out of bed
I'm not sure —
image of someone helping me back
whispering to return

I rest in the centre of the bed
alone, afraid, wary of the slightest noise
believe I'm on the wraparound porch
summer light and evening coming
August 1958 maybe —
calm, content but confused

It is *now*, it is not *then* —

Why is everyone gone?
Why am I alone?
Do I only imagine I hear voices so familiar?

I climb back into the darkness
and cling to what I think is real —
I see the nurses move through
bands of light from open doors

and the room is asleep

Why am I alone?
Why is everyone leaving?

I crouch at the edge of the bed
I only have questions —
my open palms plead for answers

3

Days later, I am back home from the hospital
— a day before Christmas Eve
my son has sawed down the tree
from our backyard
It now poses in our living room
— a string of lights draped around
its lazy branches and nothing more

Somehow it seems insincere
more like a stranger in a costume
pretending to be part of the family

Sunday Best

Back then I was never so close to God
than when I stepped out of my Dad's car
every Sunday morning
ties and stiff white shirts and shoes
and hair slicked down for
Sunday best

I was closer to God back then
driving in my Dad's Plymouth
and parking in the morning sun
before the day turned humid
my youthful face gazing up
from that glossy reflection
from the buffed toes of my shoes

Back then God was closer
and ready to receive us Sunday mornings
wearing older brothers' trousers too large
and folded over and pinned at the back
spotless shirts and shiny shoes
and hair flattened down
and Hail Marys sputtering from our lips

Back then we walked in prayer
marched in our Sunday best
God was real and all around
and we craned our necks for the steeple rising
amid nearby streets where God prowled
among empty muted assembly lines
that lay beneath factory roofs
all bowing in unison to the steeple
that called us in our Sunday best

Something I Wanted to Say

I wanted to be him — that man
who arrived every summer
and layered oversized canvasses
over the bow of an aluminum boat
as carefully and delicately balanced
as a teacup and saucer on my mother's lap

and then he'd crank up the outboard motor
till it sputtered and coughed and finally erupted
like an old man waking in a start
and he'd put-put-put across the lake to the island

a solitary man who came weekends from Toronto
from an office tower, I imagined
from a life that seemed all a lie
to this moment when now he sailed at dusk
to the island and I'd stand at the shore
and stare across to his cabin or swim
in the cool cottage waters and forget
about him entirely until his return

— the aluminum boat slicing
through Muskoka's blue mist Monday mornings
canvases laid out flat over the boat
like a hunter's kill in the Fall
the oils ablaze with colour

I wanted to be him — that man
whose idea of creation was everything I yearned for
The poetry of grace and colour

I wanted to tell him this and promised I would
but sadly missed him the day he returned

Now I'd have to wait for next summer or maybe
the summer after or maybe never

Listening in the Solitude

Wordsworth called it "the inward eye" —
and photographer Robert Frank said
the eye should learn to listen before it looks

and now I sit in the middle of the backyard
at the end of summer, scan the garden
encircling me, daylilies, hostas, chrysanthemums

— nothing more than inattentive students
knowing I can't ignore them
knowing I can't teach them anything

knowing, too, I ought to listen or watch or simply
shut my eyes, maybe feel each of them finally
cheer softly in the late, late afternoon light

or maybe let my eyes open wide to hear them

The Magic of Poetry

Here's the road we take
in all the hapless wandering
Beneath the sun the moon the sky
Here's the way to mind
the stars that fill the lake

Here's all we need for wandering
knowing there's a melody in this journey
a song to gather voices
where words bring us closer
and take us far
where our limbs, like branches, stretch
to catch the metaphors

Here's all we need for wandering
We have words and yearnings
and feel ourselves stretch to catch the night
and see the morning rise
Here's all we need to nudge the melody beneath our feet
to take us far and find the magic
In all that lives beneath the sun the moon the sky

On First Hearing Gordon Lightfoot

Maybe the spring of 1967
on a cool Saskatchewan night
I was pacing the edge of the highway
daydreaming those flat open fields

maybe praying under an ink-black sky
that rested solitary and present over me
like the palm of a hand

when a preacher swerved
to the side of the road
in a dusty green Plymouth Belvedere

I spotted the flashing red of the ribbon style taillights
that wrapped around the knife edge crease
running down to the bumper
and heard the man shout if I needed a ride

I hopped in, eager to be on my way
and talk soon turned to Jesus
and forgiveness and morality
and the Psalms
and I asked if he could turn on the radio

That's when I first heard that voice
sailing up and out this preacher's car —
a voice that spun in the still prairie air
the blur of notes like the landscape
whistling by

and I told him to turn up the radio
and that he'd have to stop talking and listen
and said if the apostles had this man's voice
there'd be real hope to cling to

and we wound the windows shut
and grew silent in that sudden moment
seeing the highway stretch clean and straight
beneath us like endless prayer

and maybe the dashboard lit up
like a votive lamp — I'm not sure

but we fell silent and alone as
that voice in the wilderness
carried us somewhere different
somewhere distant

New Winter Shoes

Today I am wearing a new pair of shoes
— for winter, snug and waterproof and warm
and I am walking into the woods at the edge
of the city so late in the day

darkness just beginning and I think
of Ralph Waldo Emerson saying
if you have worn out your shoes
the strength of the shoe leather passes
into the fiber of your body

and how you measure health by the number
of shoes and hats and coats you have worn out
— well, there's still life in these
my new winter boots

I am feeling born again and years to go —
and still so many more winters to walk

Rainbow

for Katie Dunn

She wears a rainbow
under her right eye
one that remembers a left hook
— there and gone in an instant
one that remembers the sound
as her face turned slightly
to catch the red glove
a mere blur and glow burning and
and trailing away from her grasp

Where did it come from?

Her body instinctively dancing back
swaying and dipping and moving
yet its rhythm suddenly off
knowing those red shoes dance beneath her
out of sync with the music that throbs
in the orbital bone of her right eye

Flying Man

I met a man who said he could fly
claimed we all possessed it within us
— we simply never paid attention

but if we wished —
we could lift, and sail above barns and silos
and streetcars and neighbourhood rooftops

If we wished, we could happily
abandon a busy metropolitan street
and swoon over the brief-case morning rush

It was possible

Magic boots? No. Complicated riggings
of fanned-out wings? No. Motorized contraptions
fastened to our arms? Nope. It was in our bones
in our flesh, in our blood, our know-how
our feet, our spine, our fingers
our lightness of being

It was possible

One morning this man led me from the attic
to the rooftop of his house in the west end
and asked me if I would let myself go
tiptoe to the shingled edge, and hover over
the pool and deck chairs and patio below

I perched there, barefoot beside him on the roof
my eyes studying a maze of fences and chimneys

and air conditioners, spying children board
school buses, women pulling back
bedroom curtains to let in the sun, listening
to the city coming alive
and the man said, "Go for it."

It was possible

Here was a man who said he could fly
claimed we needed to believe in ourselves
— nothing more, nothing less

I simply needed to step off that roof

It was possible

I finally turned to him and said
"Show me how."

Nude Swimming Rules

They have banned nude swimming
at the Abbey of Gethsemani in Kentucky

— new rules, you tell me
no more late morning walks

no longer stripping off sweaty clothes
after long morning hikes
to slowly slip into a cool pond
and push out under a luminous blue sky
far from the hum of Highway 31E

But how will we manage this when
we hear the wood thrush's call
and spot bathing suits draped
like Christmas ornaments
over the low branches of the magnolias
in the grove beside the pond

I'm fine with the old rules

A Monk's Petition

I keep losing
car keys, a watch, my hat
a book, pen, wallet
It doesn't matter —
there's always St. Anthony

Please come around
Something's lost
And can't be found

Then imagine the poor monk
exhausted and fed up
finally shouting
"Hey! Find your own shit, man!"

The Priest with the Truck

The white pickup truck we drove
made me car sick as Father Bill struggled
through a cacophony of grinding gears
and four-letter words to prompt and
push this battered vehicle ever higher
into the mountains, so it was best
to sit or brace myself in the open air
feeling every jolt as we roared
along the twisted road, swerving

and ascending our way ever farther
from the Zana Valley to the Andes
closer to God, maybe closer to something
better, something other than hope
sure, call it Salvation and it was in that moment
villagers poured out into the road
waving us down, demanding us to stop
telling us an old woman was dying and
needed prayers, and so we stopped

and promptly clambered out of the truck
and slipped past a threadbare curtain
draped across the entrance and now
were idling in a dark room, the clay
stone floor cool to the feet, the mother's
eyes heavenward, tiny, crippled hands
collapsed on her chest, and Father slipped
a small vial of pure olive oil from his pocket
and in seconds was making the sign
of the cross with his thumb on her forehead

Father Mike

In memory of Father Mike Dalton

His threadbare army tunic hung
from a picture hook on the wall in
a room brimming with religious icons
rosaries and holy pictures but none of that
seemed important when he started talking

this Catholic priest, the most decorated padre
of the Canadian Army, now slumped in
a wheelchair, his legs had given out
and he prayed God would give him back
the strength to stand again

this same fellow who landed at Normandy in 1944
and drove to the front and rigged up
a makeshift altar on the hood of his Jeep
and said mass for the soldiers — they stood
by the hundreds, heads bowed
silent in the muddy earth, hours before
running into battle

this Catholic priest, still wearing the Roman collar
loved to talk, loved people, loved life, loved God
loved being a soldier, loved being a priest
and if there was anything he didn't like
it was losing those fathers and sons to war

and it mattered nothing if the orders were
to stay clear of enemy lines — instead
he listened to his own heart, sometimes sitting there

in an open Jeep — a windshield festooned
with flowers – and hear the laboured
confessions of terrified soldiers

Somehow, he feared nothing, believed
he was invincible figured he had a purpose
a reason to be, and felt lucky and said
How else do you explain how my Jeep was sprayed
with shrapnel twice, and all the men around me
died? I couldn't even get a cold!

The old priest died at the age of 107 —
and still pinned to his tunic in his room
was the medal from King George VI
— and so the story goes
in that grand moment at Buckingham Palace
Father Mike dug deep into his pockets
and proudly offered the King
a tiny tin medal of the Sacred Heart of Jesus

Winter Deer

This morning I fell flat on my face
stumbling through snowy underbrush
the toe of my boot catching on ground vines
and that sent me flying —

and when I looked up
there they were — four white-tail deer
standing so still and quiet
in the tall grass along the creek
maybe laughing at me

I found myself stupidly apologizing
for intruding, interrupting their morning
but they didn't seem to care
— they just moved on

I had nothing more to say

No Questions Asked

for Maureen

I was a boy peering out the window
and there you were stepping out from a VW Beetle
Manitoba St., Bracebridge, Ont. 1960

That was first time I saw you—
first moment I saw your smile

And I spotted my brother hurrying
around the side of the car
to take your hand in that first moment
to meet our family
He was so much taller
and you so petite
but you, so much more in command

I was a boy looking out the window
wondering about this stranger
wondering about this young woman
a young teacher, we were told
Irish Catholic and opinionated
or so my father had speculated
under his breath
worried sick over his first son
talking of marriage

There she was, now striding into our house
as if it were her own
and a smile that brightened the high-ceiling rooms

her eyes darting about sizing us all up
entirely confident, instantly connecting

All these years later, today
it is that first moment I treasure
— the smile and sway of your arrival
all wit, and laughter and embrace
in an instant of first impressions

All these years later, the thing a boy notices
is a big brother reaching for her hand
one more time to guide her into a room
of hellos, knowing in this awkward moment
that somehow in all the stillness of memory
she'll always be there with us

No questions asked

The Cure

I was not quite six years old
and I stepped out onto Ouellette Avenue
trailing my father, my tiny hands shading
my eyes from the dazzling sun
after my very first eye exam

I started wearing glasses two days later
and they rested unnaturally on my nose
like a sparrow dreaming of flying off
somewhere soon —

what followed were years
of schoolyard fights and cracked lenses
snapped temples, broken bridges, missing screws
and my father warning me he'd let me go blind
if I didn't care for them any better

But my brother cooked up a cure
in a comic book from the body builder
Charles Atlas, the man who claimed
to rip up a New York phone book in half
bend an iron rod into a horseshoe shape
with his bare hands, and now boasted
of curing blindness

and so my brother offered to lower me slowly
into the well at my grandfather's farm
near Stony Point and there I'd slip
into the cold deep expanse, wearing only a bathing suit
open my eyes wide under water for a minute
and a half — and that's all there was to it

I was terrified — I was six
my head was swimming in doubts, if the rope
snapped or my brother lost his grip
I couldn't swim, I'd never get out

and so instead he calmly led me to the farmyard
to the well near the chicken coop
and pumped the handle till water gushed
and filled a rounded and wide tin pan
that rested on the ground, and told me
to take in a deep, deep breath, dip my face
eyes open wide, into the water
and he'd count down the time
for the cure to happen

but he kept pushing my head down
my eyes staring into the scratched surface
of the basin, then finally lifted my face
from the frigid well water, and I scanned
the farmyard, saw the red blur of the hen house
and a zigzagging clothesline wavering
in the windy yard, and my dad's car
near the front steps of the farmhouse

and my brother clowning about nearby
laughing his head off —

I'd wear glasses for the rest of my life

Autumn COVID at Eagle Lake, South River

We are not out of it, not yet, not soon
happily finding the moments, the sun
and dawn drifting in across the lake

I watch my son at the end of the dock
the final day of summer with cottagers gone
and the lake rousing awake in the mist

Our lives now so bewildered by rhetoric
that it's good to be here, safe to step into
this horizon so full of autumn's colour

We are not out of it, not yet, not soon
but my son lets the lake bid him close
lets it confess its secrets, its easy warmth

over passing days when we are not
out of it, not now, not yet, not soon

DANCING TREES

Good Day Moon

Good morning, moon
a good day greeting along
this river wide with welcome

my eyes scanning your shimmering face
that rests above a towering city
waking now so late

But why are you still there —

Sister Sun is rising nearby
her light soaring in praise
to beauty and grace
easing goodbye to a dark night

So, why are you still there —

I say hello
and walk the river way
knowing I won't have you long

Good morning, moon
Good day

Dancing Trees in Ojibway

for my grandchildren

It is not quite summer, but the trees
are already dancing under a stormy sky
and this is good, I would tell my grandchildren
if they were nearby, but I walk alone

it would sound wise, probably
or if they start reading Hemingway
they would see the influence
or see that it's true, the trees *are* dancing

and that is good, and they stretch and move
with poise and grace in a time that calls
for this little bit of joy in a time that tells me
there is something better, in a time

when being alone really means this is good
this is a time to pause, to stop me in my tracks
and let me see their young limbs dancing
beneath all that is stormy, all that is alone

The Month Before
Our Daughter's Birth

for Elise

winter gardens, broken backyard fences
garbage cans, empty clotheslines

as we head home
along this tangle of alleys

exploring the months
leading up to our daughter's birth

now you are wrapped in a bright poncho
under a short black coat

We sing her birth, we hear her wish

what little money we have left
now spent on the *Sunday New York Times*
and our bellies warm from hot coffee

I remember it all —
our breath in the cold day
panting out disappearing ghostly figures

a silent prayer
in our hearts
to sing her birth
honour a wish borne

over a summer by the river
long behind us

only a memory

our car forever refusing to start —
and so we go on foot to peer into the lives of
others who know nothing of us

We sing her birth, we hear her wish

climb three flights of this slanted-ceiling home
towering above a checkerboard of rooftops
this attic view of a sleepy morning city beyond

kitchen windows, cold floors, incense
bright cupboards, and scattered notebooks

into this we bring our daughter home
a place of curled flowered wallpaper
and newspapers to fill our morning

We sing her birth, we hear her wish

and see just beyond
this chimneyed landscape
with its wavering arms of smoke
chanting *Hallelujah* for each new day

We sing her birth, we hear her wish

The First Days of Children

Elise

The day you were born
the car started
for the first time that winter
and I was able to take you home
bundled up in the boot
of your mom's
royal blue sports Austin Healey
The next day —
and for the rest of that winter
I couldn't, for the life of me
get the car started again —
but we weren't going anywhere
We kept you warm and safe
on the third floor, the attic
of that tall house on Dougall Ave
and we held you in the morning light
of that slanted ceiling tiny kitchen
overlooking the rooftops of the city
so snug and content in the months following
and it mattered nothing
if the car refused to start

André

We rose in the still darkness of dawn
tiptoeing down the wooden stairs
of your grandmother's house
— everyone still asleep
and made our way to the car

slowly edging into
this sleepy September day
It was as if you didn't want to be here
idling away well past your time
in your mother's womb
unwilling to be a part of this
content to stay put —
but it was time
and you moved into life
as if you had done this before
with all the grace of wisdom and certainty

Stéphane

Late October and
two days after my birthday
when the doctor held you up
in the harsh glare of that room
and it was your hands I saw first —
tiny and cupped as if struggling
in slow motion to grasp
some fleeting and invisible molecule
on this, your first day on earth
so determined and fierce
Nothing more perfect and beautiful

Gabriel

When people ask where you got your
name, I tell them how we had
a dozen names for you
and argued all summer over them
till that day in September —
the first day of school

for the rest of the world
and there you were
fighting to free yourself
of the umbilical cord
snaked around your neck
as you emerged on this planet
and maybe it was a good guess
maybe it was all the giving and taking
all summer long over names
Your mother saw it differently
Maybe it was an angel

Three-year-old Granddaughter
on a Summer Dock

for Vivi

You dance in summer sunlight
a little girl wearing a sparkly tutu on a wooden dock
in a lake so dark and blue
and I wonder why it is I have not written
and wonder about your journey across an ocean
and wonder about the words
that soar about you so unfamiliar
You stand in a summer now
a little girl whose gestures light up the day
and I wonder what it is about you
that has kept me so silent
Maybe it's the words I cannot find
Maybe it's the summer long past that reminds me
I cannot hold on to such shimmering moments
as you pirouette and praise the summer warmth
I see you silhouetted on a sunlit dock
in a lake so dark and blue
a little girl sashaying in a sparkly tutu
and see you whirl in a moment so pure and silent
yet still hear the forest all around clamour and commend
your playful moment till the sky melts into stillness
into a lake so dark and blue

The Magic Wand

for Lucien

The wizard is poised in the room
like a Halloween witch
with that wide-brimmed peaked hat
prattling on like a philosopher
inviting us to feel that invisible ball of energy
vibrating between our outstretched hands

She's here for the launch of the new Harry Potter book
but my five-year-old grandson is lost
in the magic wand she has placed in his hands
as she speaks about drawing protectives circles
casting spells, warding off dark forces
even banishing bunions

My grandson marvels at this instrument
whispering feverishly "Abracadabra…abracadabra…"
— no longer hearing this wizard
who has fashioned this shaman's wand
from an aging oak tree

Instead, he's channeling his own energy into the room
but it isn't working, nothing is flying about
no sudden gusts of wind, nor pantry doors
slamming shut, nor teacups rattling in mid air

and nothing bigger than he might imagine:
still poverty, still a need for world peace
still violence and pestilence and polluted lakes

My grandson is poised and ready
And frantically waves the wand about him
like a symphonic conductor gone mad

yet nothing changes — it won't even silence
this nattering witch from telling us
about Greco Roman wands
or ceremonial fire wands and lotus wands
or those used by the freemasons in
all their ritualistic nonsense
Then suddenly in a dramatic abracadabra ending
my grandson shatters the spell:
"Hey, lady, how does this thing work?"

Portrait of a City in a Pandemic

for Violette

My four-year-old granddaughter drew a picture of home —
the sky a thin blue line running along the top
of the page, the ground or soil far below

another thin line and everything in between filled
with houses and grocery stores and gas stations
and gardens and maybe a hundred lanky daylilies

stretching nearly the height of our house
and people everywhere on the street, skinny figures
racing about and the sun blinking awake

in the sliver of blue wondering why no one
is paying any attention and there's also the moon
fallen asleep on the roof of another house

and there's my granddaughter ambling along
our street, wearing a mask, and if you look closely
she's painted a smiling sun on it, alive and happy

For you, Achille,
my Newest Grandson

I am an ocean away, and have never seen you
except on my iPad, your tiny face exploring
an array of faces encircling your every sound
bright eyes ever curious of a pathway to routine
in a new world, far beyond nine months

in amniotic comfort and safety
I will see you and your sister soon enough
and for now, consider your birth, the regal name
that connects us to the Greek hero
of the Trojan War, Homer's greatest warrior

but oddly much prefer to think of Claude Debussy
how everyone called him 'Achille' and how
the sounds of his piano came alive when
he was barely seven, and today as I drive
along a gleaming summer lake near Stoney Point

in the morning light I think of that name
and maybe no one knows it also rings of settlements
along lakes and rivers, of old steepled villages
of days long past, of families making their way
across an ocean with Champlain, of Jesuit fathers

men, women, and children finding homes
along sheltered sandy shorelines, of clearing the land
cutting down trees to build churches and schools
and planting pear trees and wheat and making a life
here on this side of the ocean, awaiting your arrival

In that Bed

In the COVID Ward

Seventeen days in the COVID Ward —
two other men my brother shared the room with
died while he himself with laboured breathing
put his hands over his ears so as to deaden
the all-night screaming of a woman in the room
next to his who struggled and panicked
for air, and he wondered about himself
puzzled over where he might wind up
and times when he pleaded for a priest
yet no one ever came, or when he dreamt
he was home, only to find out he was still
curled up in a hospital bed with others
all around him dying, and times when
for hours he couldn't sleep — the only sound, a noisy
ventilator keeping the man next to him alive
but never did anyone come to say goodbye

We Are Safe

Each day these past few months
begins in muted mingling of light
and darkness, and from our windows

run the widening empty streets
of stillness and silence, and we are safe
in this persistence, and feel the sky

tumble over the city's rooftops
while we huddle, quiet and alone with
our closest, thanking our lucky stars

The Bed

We chose this moment now
to change the bed, the linens, the blankets
but also to flip the mattress end to end
and that's when we disagreed over
which way was which —

I'm saying all we need to do is
slide the mattress up and over the footboard
angle, then twist it into place
but my wife is saying it must go the other way
flip it back and twist it the opposite direction
I patiently explain what just occurred
when we together edged the mattress up and over
and how it landed on the floor
From that, it's clear what we need to do

It's not the case, she tells me

and so the negotiations persist
and the mattress sits resting against
the footboard of this Victorian bed frame
abandoned like an unwanted orphan

"What does it matter?" I say
"It's like rotating tires!" my wife says
"And so we're going to get more miles
out of this mattress?" I say sarcastically
To which she retorts "Not with you in it."

So with that, we huff and we puff and we edge
the beast back into place because

I've given in, knowing full well that
if we flip it like a coin toss, I'll be the loser
Yet I still need to say "What does it matter?
"It better matter!" says my wife, reminding me that
in a single mattress there's a swarm
of eight million dust mites unnoticed
to the naked eye — to which
I respond, "It's a matter of perspective isn't it?"

The Robin's Nest

I thought the bird's nest
would make great kindling
this cold afternoon, first of December
— the nest having tumbled
months ago from its safety
tucked in an elbow of an eavestrough

I had left it sitting there
on the back steps
feeling a little shame maybe
for even thinking I ought to toss it away

And so, it sat ignored till now
for who am I to sweep away
someone's birthplace
who am I to dismiss its future

Today is a cold one, a storm
is rousing over the lake and empty fields
and I fetch firewood and cuttings
from a summer collection of cardboard boxes
in the yard, then spot the robin's nest

It makes no sense to leave it there —
no bird will lift its halo-shaped weave
back into place to wait out the winter
It makes no sense to walk past it
arms weighted down with apple wood
and bundles of magnolia trimmings

It makes no sense to leave it there —
and I make the fire and it catches well
the chimney flue breathing up all that
summer warmth — it makes no sense
to have left it there

But there it is, just beyond in the cold rain
that comes with December's certainty

Words We Give

What words we give
What words we have
What words we use
to make the reasons

We give each other
the time, the space
We give each other
the truth, the lies

but lies are not the
words we make

We make the truth
To make it live
We make the stories
To make them real

The truth lies
in all that we find
in all the words, all the joy
that give us time

that give us now

So write your story
tell me your name
tell me your place
make me feel the colour
of your words

to give us now

Geometry of Talk

I hated fractions, anything
in halves or quarters or thirds
fractured numbers, divisions, broken bits
chaos masquerading behind logical forms

my childhood mind worried itself sick —
confounded and bewildered

how could a perfectly good number
now suddenly split apart
make any sense

and what's to puzzle over a world
of denominators and numerators

what's all this talk of the number
of equal parts being counted
or the number of parts in the whole

my childhood was ruled by fractions
tangled with distress and obsession
as I pushed numbers apart like splitting
the alphabet into smaller chunks
in search of the right word

I hated fractions — proper, improper, or mixed
finding them like faces in a mirror
or on the back of my hand
or suddenly leaping from crossword puzzles —
numbers laughing crazily at my expense

The Voices

It is morning. It is any day. It is every day
and the voices we hear are those on
radio, television, newspapers—politicians
journalists, talk show hosts, advertisers, people
with opinions, selling something or stories
or news, sometimes grim and real
sometimes eager and funny, and we listen
in the midst of a lockdown
where the only regular visitor
to stop by is Canada Post

and the two of us, now in our 70s
sit and read the paper, sip mugs of hot tea
and wonder about a time that has stretched
from the cold days of last spring to now
where we find ourselves cycling
back to when all this began

It is morning. It is any day. It is every day
and the voices after a while become
our friends, the familiar, part of a routine
we are unwilling to let go, the everyday
words and stories that we pull on
like an old sweater and we listen or
sometimes half listen, knowing our hearts
sometimes turn to believing what
spring will bring us, when the first shoots
of new life begin to show in the yard

A Certain Truth

Who can tell the truth
when it matters most?
Who matters most
when the truth is told?

Where's the truth
in all that's silent
among a room
of gathered men and women
sitting side by side?

We see it
in the language that tells
a different story
We see it in the story
that soars above those
in this crowded room
And we hear
the truth that's told

Or hear the questions
we ask ourselves
Or sense a silence
that says *why*
tell a story that's true?
And *why* stay true

A Question

The lake is a meadow in the open air
and I swim its easy movement
its undulating perfection
searching for morning quietude

a reason
to be alone, to be free

yet now sense a swell and urgency
in the water, subtle resistance to anything
I might feel

I swim in its movement in a lake
that opens its arms to reflections
where tree limbs and clouds now drift
where solitude is a question

I move under a sky that pretends it's a lake
and tells me I am a swimmer
alone and wary

I glide in this meadow in the open air
I am a question that needs a reply
I am a swimmer lost as I feel
my way through a cumulus collage

I move with the ease of the lake
listening to its urgings, sensing its demands
I swim alone, I ask for nothing
knowing this is all a lie

The Red Tulips

I wait for the morning sun
let it slip in past the fence and trees
silent and alone, past the windowpanes
and see it reach for the coffee mug

two red tulips now brighten with its grasp
and wonder if this is how we ought
to meet each day, wonder if this is how
we ought to surrender to its warmth

Warmth in that Moment

for Donna

Every morning I am up at the same time
making tea, dropping two slices
of bread into the toaster, scooping up
the paper at the front door

and settling down into a chair
at the kitchen table to read the news
sip a hot cup and gather
my thoughts, but before long

I head back to sleep, slide
in beside my wife, seeking the warmth
of her body on this cold morning
in late October and soon after

she pulls back the blankets on her side
sits up and steals out of the quiet, pauses
to put on her slippers and silently tiptoe
around the end of the bed and out the room

and in that moment now alone
I find myself slip into the warmth
she has left, like a lone swimmer
finding a patch of sun in a cold lake

Acknowledgements

There are so many to thank for the support given to me over the years but let me name a few that come to mind: Rosemary Sullivan, Robert Hilles, John B. Lee, Phil Hall, Karen Mulhallen, Nino Ricci, Douglas Glover, Nadine Deleury, Dan Wells, Peter Hrastovec, Roger Bryan, Josh Canty, Julienne Rousseau, D.A. Lockhart, Micheline Maylor, André Narbonne, Alicia Labbé, Douglas MacLellan, Laurence Hutchman, Mary Ann Mulhern, Christopher Menard, Roger Bell, and Susan McMaster. A big thank you to Heather McCardell and KC Santo for proofreading this manuscript and making some valuable suggestions I am especially grateful to Bruce Meyer who found a way to knit these poems into a collection that serves a better purpose than what I might've dreamed up. A big shout-out to Howard and Jeannette Aster for all their support and friendship over the years, the great conversations, the best food in Burgundy, the fondest memories of staying at La Roche D'Hys — a place that truly inspires poets and artists and musicians. Finally, it goes without saying that I am profoundly blessed with my wife, Donna, who clearly understands my necessity to daydream and fall asleep on the couch in the middle of imagining many more new poems.

About the Author

Marty Gervais is an award-winning journalist, poet, playwright, historian, photographer, and editor, and served as the City of Windsor's first Poet Laureate. In 1996, he was awarded the Milton Acorn People's Poetry Award for his Mosaic Press book, *Tearing Into A Summer Day*. This book also was granted the City of Windsor Mayor's Award for literature. In 1998, he won the prestigious Toronto's Harbourfront Festival Prize for his contributions to Canadian letters and to emerging writers. In 2003, Gervais was given the City of Windsor Mayor's Award for literature for *To Be Now: Selected Poems*, another Mosaic Press title. His most successful work, *The Rumrunners*, a book about the Prohibition period, was a Canadian bestseller and was on the top ten Globe and Mail bestseller list for non-fiction titles. Another book, *Seeds In The Wilderness*, stemmed from interviews Gervais conducted with such notable religious leaders as Mother Teresa, Bishop Desmond Tutu, Hans Kung, and Terry Waite.